RING-TAILED LEMURS

MARYSA STORM

BLACK
RABBIT
BOOKS

Bolt Jr. is published by Black Rabbit Books
P.O. Box 3263, Mankato, Minnesota, 56002.
www.blackrabbitbooks.com
Copyright © 2020 Black Rabbit Books

Catherine Cates, designer; Omay Ayres, photo researcher

Names: Storm, Marysa, author.
Title: Ring-tailed lemurs / by Marysa Storm.
Description: Mankato, Minnesota : Black Rabbit Books, [2020] | Series: Bolt Jr. Awesome animal lives | Audience: Age 6-8. | Audience: K to Grade 3. | Includes bibliographical references and index.
Identifiers: LCCN 2018053278 (print) | LCCN 2018055081 (ebook) | ISBN 9781623101602 (e-book) | ISBN 9781623101541 (library binding) | ISBN 9781644661048 (paperback)
Subjects: LCSH: Ring-tailed lemur–Juvenile literature.
Classification: LCC QL737.P95 (ebook) | LCC QL737.P95 S76 2020 (print) | DDC 599.8/3–dc23
LC record available at https://lccn.loc.gov/2018053278

Printed in the United States. 5/19

Image Credits
Alamy: BIOSPHOTO, 8–9; Jonathan Mbu (Pura Vida Exotics), 22–23; Paul Thompson Images, 6–7; iStock: Tamascsere, 5; Shutterstock: Aaron Amat, 21; Agami Photo Agency, 13; alexavol, 7; Animalvector, 15; Anna Phillips, 1; Arto Hakola, 20–21; ATTILA Barsan, 12–13; Daleen Loest, Cover; Edward Hasting-Evans, 10–11; e'walker, 10; iop_micro, 3, 24; Iryna Art, 16–17, 17; Marcella Miriello, 18–19; mariait, 4; photo by clemma, 16–17; yod67, 14

Contents

CHAPTER 1

A Day in the Life

Ring-tailed lemurs climb through leafy trees. They leap from branch to branch. They're looking for bugs. They eat any they find. The lemurs then drop to the ground. They stretch out. It's time to **sunbathe**.

sunbathe: to sit or lie in the sun's light

ring-tailed lemur ◄ ·······

up to 8 pounds
(4 kilograms)

WEIGHT COMPARISON

Long Tails

Ring-tailed lemurs spend a lot of time in trees. Their long tails help them balance. Their name comes from the tails' rings.

► American shorthair cat
up to 15 pounds
(7 kg)

7

Ring-Tailed Lemur

ears

nose

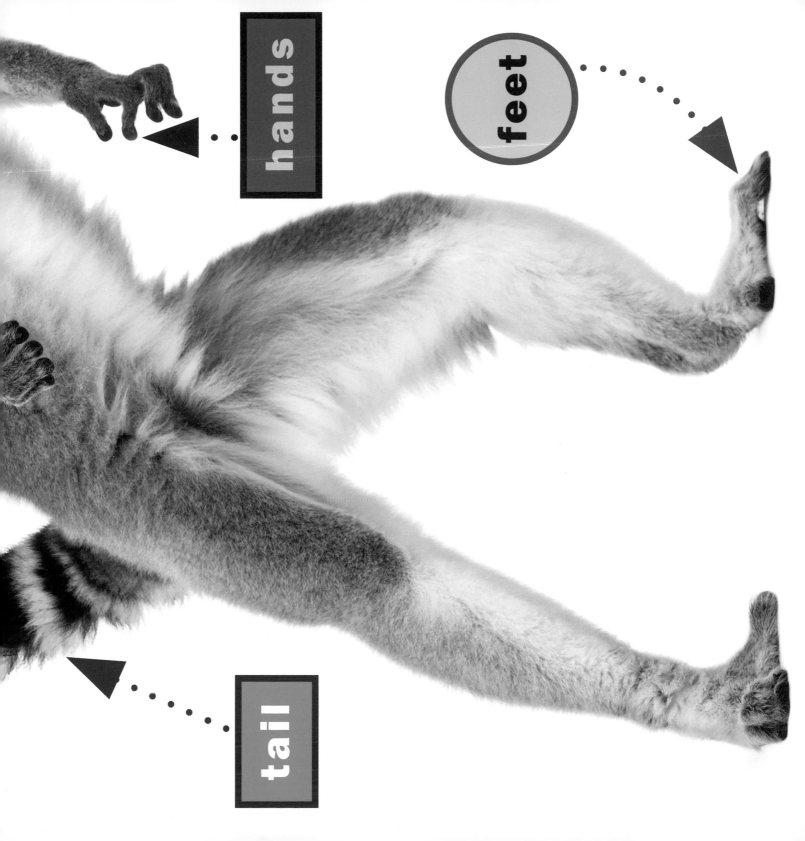

hands

feet

tail

CHAPTER 2

Food and Homes

Ring-tailed lemurs eat fruit. They also eat leaves and flowers. **Insects** make good meals too.

insect: a small animal that has six legs

11

Their Homes

Lemurs live on Madagascar. It's an **island** near Africa. Lemurs live in its forests. They make their homes in the trees.

island: an area of land surrounded by water

Where Ring-Tailed Lemurs Live

Africa

Madagascar

KEY

■ = where ring-tailed lemurs live

CHAPTER 3

Family Life

Ring-tailed lemurs live in troops. Troops have about 15 lemurs. Males and females live together. One female leads each group.

FACT

Lemurs clean each other.

Babies

Females usually have one baby at a time. Mothers keep their babies safe. They also show them what to eat. Young lemurs soon become strong. After about six months, they care for themselves.

Newborn Ring-Tailed Lemur's Body Length
about 4 inches
(10 centimeters)

Bonus Facts

Ring-tailed lemurs live about 16 years.

Mothers help each other raise their babies.

Their tails are about 2 feet (1 meter) long.

Ring-tailed lemurs can purr.

purr: a low, soft sound

READ MORE/WEBSITES

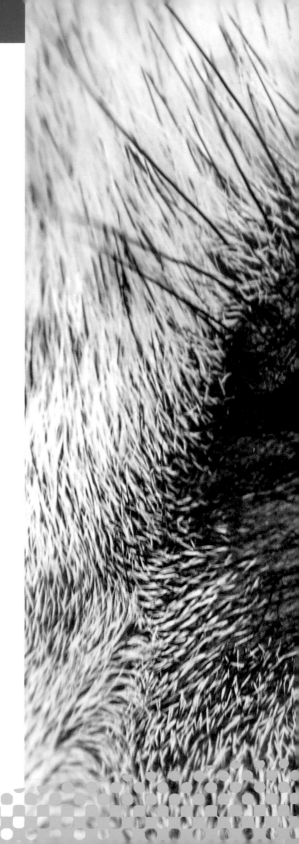

Bodden, Valerie. *Lemurs.* Amazing Animals. Mankato, MN: Creative Education, 2019.

Dicmas, Courtney. *Lemur Dreamer.* Tulsa, OK: Kane Miller, a division of EDC Publishing, 2018.

Terp, Gail. *Ring-Tailed Lemurs.* Wild Animal Kingdom. Mankato, MN: Black Rabbit Books, 2018.

Ring-Tailed Lemur
kids.nationalgeographic.com/animals/ring-tailed-lemur/#ww-madagascar-animals-ring-tailed-lemurs.jpg

Ring-Tailed Lemur
kids.sandiegozoo.org/animals/ring-tailed-lemur

GLOSSARY

insect (IN-sekt)—a small animal that has six legs

island (AHY-luhnd)—an area of land surrounded by water

purr (PUR)—a low, soft sound

sunbathe (SUHN-beyth)—to sit or lie in the sun's light

INDEX